KU-036-118

The Little Book of
Bhāvanā

The Thai secrets
of everyday resilience

DR LEAH WEISS

Quercus

First published in Great Britain in 2019 by

Quercus Editions Ltd
Carmelite House
50 Victoria Embankment
London EC4Y 0DZ

An Hachette UK company

Copyright © 2019 Leah Weiss

The moral right of Leah Weiss to
be identified as the author of this work has been
asserted in accordance with the Copyright,
Designs and Patents Act, 1988.

All rights reserved. No part of this publication
may be reproduced or transmitted in any form
or by any means, electronic or mechanical,
including photocopy, recording, or any
information storage and retrieval system,
without permission in writing from the publisher.

A CIP catalogue record for this book is available
from the British Library

HB ISBN 978 1 52940 068 7
Ebook ISBN 978 1 52940 067 0

Every effort has been made to contact copyright holders.
However, the publishers will be glad to rectify in future
editions any inadvertent omissions brought to their attention.

Quercus Editions Ltd hereby exclude all liability to the extent
permitted by law for any errors or omissions in this book and for any loss,
damage or expense (whether direct or indirect) suffered by a
third party relying on any information contained in this book.

10 9 8 7 6 5 4 3 2 1

Illustrations by Amber Anderson
Text designed and typeset by CC Book Production
Printed and bound in Great Britain by Clays Ltd, Elcograf S.p.A.

To my late father, Dr Andrew B. Weiss, who taught me the power of human resilience and the importance of asking life's big questions. I miss you every day.

'No one saves us but ourselves.
No one can and no one may.
We ourselves must walk the path'

The Buddha

Contents

Preface   1

An Introduction to *Bhāvanā*   9

I   *Citta-Bhāvanā*: Clarity   15

II   *Samādhi-Bhāvanā*: Attention   39

III *Kāya-Bhāvanā*: Embodiment   57

IV   *Mettā-Bhāvanā*: Compassion   77

V   *Paññā-Bhāvanā*: Wisdom   97

Afterword: My Meditation Guide   113

Acknowledgements   135

Preface

For most of us, life is built around routines. We go about our daily business repeating the same patterns, generally speaking – whether it's our commute to and from work, our adherence to a bedtime schedule that ensures we and our children develop good sleeping habits (hopefully), or the way we unwind with our friends and partners at the weekend. We know the sun will come up in the morning and go down at night. We don't expect things to change dramatically. We worry about this, delight in that, but generally we just trundle along, in a kind of sleepwalking state.

We know enough about neuroscience to understand why we do this. Our brains have created shortcuts that allow us to navigate our daily activities with as little effort as possible. We do things without thinking. Ignoring details about the environment around us and specifics about our internal experiences is an energy-conservation method that the human brain has evolved to employ. This has turned into our default way of living.

This technique, while efficient, can cause us to miss key moments to stop, take stock and notice. We miss the opportunity to learn from our personal processes in thought and behaviour, and that is an issue.

What happens when life presents an unexpected challenge? Sometimes it's a small thing, an inconvenience, such as spilling a cup of coffee all over our laptop or a close call with the bollard that was in our blind spot as we reversed out of the car park. In these situations, we are forced to reassess things and do some quick thinking to try to restore order.

But at other times we encounter major shake-ups for which there is no quick fix: a surprise redundancy, the unexpected loss of a friend, or maybe a diagnosis that turns our world upside down.

When such an event hits us with full force, will we have the tools we need not only to survive but to do so with calmness, dignity and even grace? Is there also a way of coping that ensures we won't suffer from any subsequent psychological trauma?

There are two crucial questions. What skills do we need to face such challenges? And, how can we develop these skills in a realistic way?

Sometimes, there are obvious practical steps we can take. Living in California and having three small children, I take the threat of wildfires and earthquakes seriously. Putting together an emergency go-bag forces me to remember the very basics that are necessary, such as food, water, clothing and cash, to keep my family and me alive.

But, as we'll see, it's the figurative emergency go-bags that we need to focus on. And we need to prepare them now. Paradoxically, a crisis can be an empowering wake-up call, forcing us to shake off our slumber and take stock of our lives.

What began as an adventure for twelve boys aged eleven to sixteen and their twenty-five-year-old soccer coach, on 23 June 2018, quickly turned ominous when they found themselves trapped in a cave known as Tham Luang, in northern Thailand. This was an unexpected setback of monstrous proportions. They had no food, no drinking water, and they faced what seemed to be inevitable death as water inside the cave rose steadily and the oxygen level dropped. After one week in the cave, the oxygen level had decreased to just fifteen per cent – a level that poses a serious risk of hypoxia, meaning death by suffocation. Whichever way you looked at it, their chances of survival seemed very slim.

Well aware of the choices he had made that had led the boys to the cave, the coach, Ekkapol Chanthawong, was determined to do everything he could to keep them alive. One of the survival tactics he employed was meditation. It might seem like a strange idea – that meditation itself would become the difference between whether the boys survived or perished – but Ekkapol knew that it would benefit the boys' ability to endure their dire circumstances. He had, after all, spent ten years training to be a Buddhist monk, and meditation was built into his daily routine.

For ten days, engineers attempted to solve the immense problem of how to extract the boys from the cave, alive. Weather, currents and limited time presented challenges that made the rescue appear implausible, if not impossible. When the divers finally made it to the chamber of the cave, on 10 July, with the world watching on television and computer screens, they found the boys either crouching on the ledge, or sitting cross-legged in silent meditation. They were weak and hungry, but they were alive.

This story is relevant because experts believe that the two elements that kept those boys alive were, firstly, the water

5

dripping inside the cave, which the boys drank, and, secondly, the meditation. And it is the meditation – the mental go-bag – that we will be exploring throughout this book, because it's something we can all learn and hugely benefit from. Indeed, the chapters that follow will help you prepare for your 'cave' – not a literal one, hopefully, but the times in your life when events feel like they're closing in on you and it's hard to breathe. When air seems scarce and anxiety takes over, using the same meditation methods that the Thai boys used will help you to find clarity, gain perspective and breathe through it.

When this story broke, I was contacted by a journalist at CNBC to elucidate the role that meditation can play during times of crisis. I talked about the physiology of meditation, how it leads to a lower heart rate, reduced oxygen consumption and to self-soothing, which allows you to keep calm and not make ill-advised mistakes in a high-pressure situation. In this book, I'll go into much more depth and demonstrate what a wonderful and powerful tool meditation can be. I will show you how meditation deployed alongside Buddhist principles and rituals that exist within the *bhāvanā* framework can be applied in everyday life, and how our attitude towards life influences both the way we live and also the way we approach death (which also has a huge impact on how we live). I'll also demonstrate how to begin a meditation practice in the context of a busy life, using accessible techniques and achievable goals.

Drawing on my years of experience on hundred-day and six-month retreats, as well as the popular course I teach on compassionate leadership at the Stanford Graduate School of Business, I'll break down the mysteriousness of meditation, Buddhist tradition and psychological research on resilience, so you, too, can benefit from these skills. And I will refer to the Thai boys' experience throughout, as there is so much there for us to learn from, following their example of how to deal with an extremely stressful situation with lucidity, calm and discipline.

Along the way, I also integrate these teachings and practices with the most recent neuroscientific theories on how our brains and behaviour patterns can change to create new experiences from familiar or habitual situations.

The good news is that a brain transplant is not required for transformation to happen. By training ourselves to be present to the small inconveniences we experience day to day, we can be ready for a big crisis when it comes.

An Introduction to *Bhāvanā*

To put it simply, *bhāvanā* is the cultivation of wisdom and tranquillity. It is the means by which we can develop the resilience and strength that will support us when our time of need arrives. It is a process of learning that helps us reconnect with our authentic selves. This book makes *bhāvanā* accessible and practical by distilling the insights of thousands of years of Buddhist tradition, and the best way to understand *bhāvanā* is through the practice of meditation.

Each chapter of this book includes a clearly defined element of *bhāvanā*, accompanied by a specific lesson on how it relates to everyday life.

There are five distinct components of *bhāvanā* to master in order to reach the goal of enlightenment, or deeply integrated wisdom. Each of these domains is crucial for mental well-being. Together, they add up to a set of resources that can make all the difference when having to cope with the challenges life throws at you.

The Five Bhāvanā Framework

1) *Citta-bhāvanā*: clarity

2) *Samādhi-bhāvanā*: attention

3) *Kāya-bhāvanā*: embodiment

4) *Mettā-bhāvanā*: compassion

5) *Paññā-bhāvanā*: wisdom

After reading about a particular *bhāvanā*, you can then explore it in your daily life, integrate it into drills that you can learn from, and ultimately develop new habits of thinking and behaviour. These five strands of *bhāvanā* are the tools you can use to wake up from the daydream of a partly engaged life, giving you a readiness to act when you need it. Just as the boys of the Thai soccer team maintained equilibrium by using their mental abilities to transition from what started as a fun adventure to what became a life-threatening situation, so you can be an agile spiritual athlete, and prepare yourself for any seismic life events that might reframe your very existence. This process, from the moment it is begun, allows us to uncover a powerful tool: the ability to find training opportunities in the most mundane aspects of daily life. Through exploring the five *bhāvanās*, we can understand what *gets in the way* of being more present in our own lives, and we can become more resilient.

Some of this will be intuitive and easily done – you might even find yourself approaching the way you do business in a decidedly different way, almost without realizing you're doing it. Most of it, though, will require significantly more attention and effort. That we all have different strengths and weaknesses in our cognitive, emotional and physical attunement is hardly surprising given complex factors such as genes, culture, experience and personality. Identifying and exploring these individual strengths and weaknesses is crucial. Buddhist teachings refer to the idea of reincarnation, and that aspects of our personality relate to prior experiences and efforts made in our lives, both the one we are living now and carried forward from previous lives as well. The idea is that we can access and activate the heartfelt devotion that our prior incarnations had, giving us the potential to live a more meaningful life.

At the end of each chapter, I have included a **Mindset Hack** section for the relevant strand of *bhāvanā*. This training suggests ways of reframing your thinking, not just when it's convenient, but every day, come rain or shine.

There is also a **Light Lift Practice** section, which includes simple, approachable tasks to help you identify the small steps you can take in your daily life as part of your training.

Together, these practices will break down the changes we must make to incorporate the five strands of *bhāvanā* into our day-to-day lives. By the end of the book, you will be well on your way to living a life enriched by resilience, strength and grace.

CHAPTER I

Citta-Bhāvanā: Clarity

'After much seeking for truth and knowledge, the profoundness of reality came to me with a clarity never known before'

The Buddha

Many of us rush from event to event with little to no blank space in our calendar. Even our to-do lists give rise to more to-do lists. That's okay, we all need some kind of structure.

The problem is, with all the swirl in our daily lives, many of us feel that we can't do everything we are meant to do. We are overwhelmed and stuck in the scarcity mindset – not enough time, not enough money, not enough *me* to go around. We feel we are failing.

We also lose track of what really matters. We spend our time accomplishing this and finishing that, but the danger is that very little of what we do is aligned with what we most want to contribute to the world or develop in ourselves as human beings. This may account for why many of us wake up in the wee hours of the morning worrying about the big things, the things that never show up on our lists.

We need proven methods to reframe our life experience, from overwhelming and distracted, into conscious lucidity. In doing so, we can live in the present and free ourselves from rehashing the past while anxiously rehearsing for the future. This enlightenment will translate into an ability to discern how to invest our time wisely and work out what matters without getting distracted by what doesn't.

Which is why the first of the *bhāvanās* is clarity: the ability to perceive with lucidity and with wisdom. Yeshe Tsogyal was the Mother of Tibetan Buddhism, and one of the songs she wrote expresses this sentiment well:

> *Every appearance and every event*
> *Are the mind's miraculous display.*
> *In the spacious expanse, I see nothing to fear.*

It is just reflexive radiance
Of mind's clear light, and nothing else.
Hence there's no reason to react.
All activity is my adornment.

THE FOUR REMINDERS

To achieve clarity, we need to reflect on the Four Reminders, which act as centring truths in the Tibetan Buddhist tradition and which clarify what is important in any given situation or on any given day. The first of these is known as the Preciousness of Human Life, in which we remember how fortunate we are to have been born at all in a world where we have the opportunity of self-reflection, learning and growth, which will take us in the direction of awakening.

The second is Impermanence, where we contemplate the reality that nothing is forever, least of all our very bodies, which are 'like a water bubble' on a stream. It is uncertain when we will die, but die we will. Life is tenuous and precious.

The third is Karma, or the idea of actions and consequences. Everything we do in life will affect not only ourselves but those around us and the world itself. This is something that is an ongoing process, and involves how we choose to respond to events in our lives and how those responses make us feel.

The fourth reminder is Samsara, or the unending cycle of life, death and rebirth, and all the suffering that entails. The only release from this cycle comes when we achieve Nirvana. In other words, Samsara is the daily grind, the tediousness of daily life, and enlightenment is a perspective shift that allows us to see the sacred within the mundane.

Appreciating that death can happen without notice is a key element of Buddhist training in any monastery. This isn't an idea that practitioners are exposed to, nod yes to and move on from. It is built into practice every single day. It is among the first and last thoughts of the day and a reflection that punctuates all activities – including the mundane. It is the foundation for finding this much-needed sense of clarity. We will only carpe our diems if we remember that we won't be around forever and we must seize the opportunity to do what matters while we can. We will prioritize impact and meaning rather than push the snooze button through a life that falsely seems like it will last forever.

When the world heard about the Thai boys' predicament in the cave, the preciousness of life and the fact that it can end without warning was brought into sharp relief. We all wondered whether they'd come out of it alive.

Confronted with this thought too, coach Ekkapol had to focus on the essentials. His ability to discern what would be a good use of limited resources – physical and mental – was crucial for survival. 'From the beginning that I knew that we were stuck in the cave, I first tried to regain my composure,' he said in an interview after they were rescued. 'I tried not to tell the boys that we got stuck in the cave. I only told them something positive. I told the boys that we just had to wait for a bit longer, then the water may go down and we could get out. I tried not to make them panic. If I told them that we got stuck in the cave, the boys would get panicked.'

And so he taught them to meditate.

THE IMPORTANCE OF MEDITATION

Ekkapol was sent to a Buddhist monastery when he was only ten years old, two years after the death of his parents and brother due to a disease that had swept through their village. He lived in the monastery as a novice monk for about a decade, learning the fundamentals of Buddhist practice and receiving an education that otherwise would have been unattainable for him.

Novice monks have fewer precepts to follow than fully ordained monks (10 rather than 227). The first step of this process is understanding what it means to 'go forth into homelessness' and renounce the comforts of life for the path of contemplation. Each step along the way is accompanied by ritual elements – wearing white for the first step, which is learning the implications of making the choice to join the monastic order as a novice, then shaving the head and changing to yellow robes once the choice to ordain has been confirmed.

From here, the monks learn the meditations and rituals that form the core of the training on a path to enlightenment. They take refuge in the Three Jewels, chanting three times, 'I take refuge in the Buddha, in the Dharma [teaching/practice], and in the Sangha [community/ancestry of practice],' words they go on to repeat many times a day. They bow three times as part of this affirmation.

And from there, they start the process of receiving offerings from the community to provide for their needs – which provides the community with an opportunity to create good karma (known as merit) by supporting the noble path of the monastics. There are numerous aspects to the discipline that these young monks follow – including no longer eating meals after lunch. They commit to following a set of other precepts: to refrain from killing, stealing, sexual acts, lying, intoxicants, singing, music, dancing and entertainment, perfume, make-up and other adornments, high chairs and non-modest bedding, and accepting money. If they continue along the path of training, eventually they will be invited into the monastic community as a full participant.

The coach knew, like all Buddhists, that meditation is a go-to when you are distressed or in danger. He might not have actually thought this through in so many words, but he instinctively knew that cognitive resources, which otherwise would be hijacked by feeling threatened or panicked, could be accessed when in a calm frame of mind to increase problem-solving capacity.

And, given that insufficient air and food was a major issue for the trapped boys, meditation was actually a very practical response to both of these concerns. Meditation, we know from vast amounts of research on the topic, helped the boys conserve oxygen and even slow their metabolism, which was critical in keeping them safe from asphyxiation and starvation in the extreme conditions of minimal food and minimal oxygen.

Through clarity, Buddhists attempt to keep their perspectives in check, becoming expert in focusing on what matters most and avoiding unhelpful reactivity that leads to poor decision-making. They know that mental states can be curated. This point will be brought home time and time again throughout the book, as perspective is literally what kept the Thai boys going.

IDENTIFYING PURPOSE

Sometimes it takes a few attempts to establish what it is you have to do. When interviewed, the boys said their intention, upon entering the cave, was to spend one hour exploring it, but when they retraced their steps, the water had risen so much it made their way out of the cave impassable. They had a clear purpose, but when circumstances changed, they had to adapt and learn to cope with their predicament.

If they had allowed fear, panic and instinct to take over, and had tried to wade out of the cave, when none of them could swim particularly well, if at all, they would have run out of resources – mental and physical – and would have been less able to comply with the daunting things that were asked of them in the demanding rescue efforts. Initially, they did try to claw their way out of the cave by scratching at the rock surfaces, but they quickly realized that was pointless, too.

When considering the neuroscience of fear and the knee-jerk reactions it can trigger, it becomes even more astonishing to consider how calm the boys remained. When we are in threat-response mode, the activity in the pain regions of our brain becomes more acute, which leads us to do rash things to make it stop. What the Thai boys did and what they were able to do was highly unusual, and it hinged on their strength in purpose and their ability to override the threat response.

Purpose is a key word here. In our own lives, it is crucial to be clear about what really matters and what does not matter. We've all had days when we've started work without intention and then have looked up at midday to find that we've been mindlessly answering pointless emails all day. With a stronger objective, we can stop wasting our precious time on non-priorities or losing battles (trying to get our inbox down to zero, for example).

Purpose long-term is important too. When we understand the difference between what happens when we pursue hedonia (passing sensory pleasures) and what happens when we pursue eudaimonia (clarifying our deeper values and staying connected to them), that's when countless opportunities for joy open up to us. Ultimately, as we'll see later, renunciation becomes a critical part of the journey.

Incidentally, renunciation does not have to mean giving away our belongings, quitting our jobs, saying goodbye to our families and heading for the mountains. It can simply mean identifying what is not a good use of our time and getting rid of that. This is the real challenge: being aware of harmful habits, however big or small they may be, and making the necessary changes to live a life free of these unhelpful distractions. In this way, we can allocate our limited energy to the right things.

Ekkapol did not let self-criticism get in the way of his purpose. He knew he couldn't waste mental resources beating himself up. He had a problem to solve, and he could not let any self-flagellation hijack his cognitive resources. Even though he was suffering himself, he was able to take action, teaching the boys to meditate to help them conserve energy and stay calm.

Self-criticism is a seductive habit. We think doing penance is beneficial, as we believe it shows we care: *See, I feel bad; I care; I am a good person.* It can even seem altruistic. But actually, self-criticism is the opposite of helpful – for us, and for those around us – certainly at times when we need to get an off-the-rails situation back on track. Our brain doesn't know the difference between someone else screaming at us and us screaming at ourselves; the threat alarms within our brains make the same sound. Self-deprecation really eats away at our ability to act in a resourceful way.

FAMILIAR STORIES

We each construct our own world, and how we construct it determines what is possible for us. One of the first ways to increase overall clarity is to recognize the ways in which personal perspectives and interpretations – our stories – are influencing our experience and behaviour.

Our minds play all kinds of tricks on us that can lead to experiencing more pain than is really necessary or helpful. The shortcuts we resort to – the actions we repeat, the mindset we engage with repeatedly – prevent us from progressing. We dig a hole and don't give ourselves the tools to get out of it.

Without proper training, it is difficult to discern the difference between what is actually happening and what our internal dialogue is telling us is happening. We become adept at selecting data that supports our pre-existing points of view. On top of that, our emotional reactions colour our rational thinking to a significant degree. Illusions are created because of our brain's automatic tendency to piece together information that creates a pattern, where in reality there may not be one. It means that our perception is not particularly trustworthy. In order to improve our clarity, we need to understand that there are forces at play within ourselves of which we may not be fully conscious.

Buddhists have recognized this problem for thousands of years. A foundational element of Buddhist meditation training is to take stock of a situation without automatically following the mind down the meandering garden path of familiar interpretation. This training leads to a heightened and direct understanding of how the mind generates full-on stories out of thin air. When we understand how this happens, then we can learn to deconstruct or cease to construct these stories. And we can live in a world more closely aligned to reality.

Clarity means understanding that we can return to the simplicity of direct experience rather than proliferating our endless thoughts, fears, and worries.

SMALL ACTIONS

We need to sharpen our capacity to pay attention. The term *mindfulness* is used broadly and includes a lot of things. At its core, it is about the intentional use of attention. As we'll see in the next chapter, paying closer attention is the only way we can change how we live our lives and construct a world that is healthy and harmonious, rather than full of dead ends and brick walls.

Clarity means that we can see when we are going off the rails, and it allows us to get back on track and take simple steps to deal with our tendency to let things unravel in a way that is unhelpful and irrelevant.

Ekkapol's clarity – getting the boys to remain calm and not panic – was what helped save the day.

This clarity comes with a lot of practice, a lot of trials and tribulations. In the process of Buddhist psychology, we start with intention setting – meaning, we clarify what we need or want. Then we do something, with this intention in mind. At the end of the process, we reflect on what worked and what went awry. We connect our efforts in these small arenas to our larger aspirations for our impact on the world and recall that we can't have a large impact without small actions. Intention, practice and dedication are processes that yogis use to structure their learning. Interestingly, this is consistent with current research on behaviour change – small, well-placed efforts make more difference than occasional grand yet unsustainable efforts.

So, let's keep in mind that epiphanies and dramatic overhauls are not the way forward. The mundane details are the frontiers of change. Don't make the all-too-common mistake of taking yourself out of the game with impossible standards for cathartic transformation that no one could meet. Instead, remember it's the small steps that matter – because these small steps actually aren't so small. They build and they build, and that is where change happens.

MINDSET HACK

Agency, or the ability to take action to influence our situation, is a core component of resilience. It is challenging to close the gaps between our values, our purpose and how we spend our time, and to put our beliefs into action. We need to identify what is happening, where our time goes and what kind of perspective we are bringing to the things that matter to us.

Work on Your Purpose

Purpose is not something we usually think about when considering our New Year's resolutions. But if we want to live lives aligned with our values, if we want to find real happiness, then purpose needs to be a continual touchpoint. Keep in mind the puzzle-box metaphor: when you're working on a jigsaw puzzle, you keep referring to the picture on the box, don't you?

Today, this hour, this minute – all matter. Any point in time can be a learning opportunity to help us nudge our actions towards being more aligned with our values. As we remember this, we can construct our days with this principle in mind. We can reclaim beauty, awe and purpose in the small moments of our lives.

Repetitive actions can be very helpful. Research shows that habits, including rituals, can act as powerful reminders of what is important to us. Religious traditions have relied on rituals for thousands of years – from the keeping of the Sabbath for Jews, to the five sessions of daily prayer for Muslims – because attaching these reminders of our values to a daily or weekly routine can help us maintain our core purpose. Incidentally, rituals don't have to be religious – it's all about finding what resonates.

Rethink Your Calendar

Calendars can reflect other people's priorities rather than our own necessities. That doesn't make calendar events bad – but it does mean that they are not a reliable indication of how to spend our time wisely. Calendars are often filled with things that we scheduled weeks ago and didn't think twice about at the time. We're all guilty of saying yes to an invitation or a meeting because it's easier than saying no, and because we haven't got the mental space to imagine how pointless or unproductive it will feel when the moment comes. The white space in your calendar is there to be filled, after all . . .

Once you've established your purpose, audit your calendar and align it with your priorities. We need to make sure that our biggest dreams have time allocated to them, and that we aren't spending time on shoulds and FOMOs rather than our core purpose. Make sure there is plenty of white to counterbalance the spaces that are already filled in. That is when you can focus on your creative pursuits and those tasks that support your dreams.

Change the Narrative

When we don't have sufficient information about what is happening around us, we create meaning. The problem is, as we have seen, this meaning is largely negative. We personalize events and other people's reactions, interpreting them as responding to us when they aren't. For example, we decide a person is judgemental because they are frowning while we talk, when we are actually missing the fact that this person always frowns when they are listening carefully. We make up a story that they dislike us, which makes us afraid of them, which means we then change our behaviour to avoid them. Why? Because negative facts make a stronger impression on us than positive or neutral ones.

This bias towards fear or paranoia does not mean we are bad people. It is rooted in the neuroscience of how our minds have evolved. We are hyper-aware of how other people respond to us because this is a strategy we have always used to stay safe. Back in the day, life and death depended on it – we couldn't survive if we were thrown out of the group.

Be aware that the thought patterns you are creating are not necessarily accurate, truthful or productive.

LIGHT LIFT PRACTICE

Look at the past seven days. Review how your time was spent and consider how much of it was on activities that really mattered to you. Were there any activities you spent time on that you would regret if this had been the last week of your life?

Now look ahead to the next week. What could you change as a result of this line of enquiry? Pick something you can add that will be meaningful and strike something off that does not move your purpose forward.

As you live your life, reflect on these ideas. Send yourself a calendar event that says, *This week could be your last*, and see what this does for you, your relationships and your priorities.

Remember, it's the small things that matter. Use specific moments in the day – a coffee break or your commute into work – to establish mini-rituals which can provide you with opportunities to remind yourself about your purpose. Try to catch when you feel yourself going astray, so you can get back on track more readily.

CHAPTER II

Samādhi-Bhāvanā: Attention

'Do not dwell in the past, do not dream of the future, concentrate the mind on the present moment'

The Buddha

You can't focus on your purpose if you're not paying attention. Even when you are meditating, you need to place your attention on an object or anchor, whether it is the breath or a visualization, to develop focus.

Outside of meditating, we can develop the capacity for focus by applying our attention to any activity, whether it is emailing, listening to a friend in distress, or diving to rescue people stranded in a cave. It fits everywhere. The ability to place our attention on a target and return to it when it strays is the cornerstone of mindfulness.

WHY WE NEED MINDFULNESS

What is mindfulness? I have thought long and hard about how to explain it, and the best definition I have come up with is this: mindfulness is the intentional use of attention. It is simple, but at the same time contains much within it.

As we all know, in the world in which we live, distraction is at an all-time high. Whether it's because of a digital calendar reminder in our inbox, a Twitter alert on our phone, a billboard advert at the Underground station or a radio jingle in our ears, our attention is fractured. We are in an attention economy, kidding ourselves into believing the myth that multitasking is the solution and will save us time, despite research pointing to the contrary.

Why don't we accept that we can't do more than one thing properly at a time? When we try to listen while catching up on emails, our minds are actually moving back and forth between things – not doing both at once. It's incredibly inefficient. Multitasking can make us feel bad because it is not as productive as we'd hoped, and it's not productive for the very good reason that it is ineffective.

How can we address this? Well, if we want to reclaim our attention, we need to acknowledge our lack of focus. The human mind is designed to be very active, and having our attention stray is normal. Cavemen and women had to be mentally agile and flexible in order to survive, as they always had to be alert to threats and dangers taking them by surprise. But, in today's world, the ease with which our attention strays isn't so much about safety as it is about habituation.

There are several emotional states that can lead to distraction. There is agitation, when our minds bounce all over the place because we simply have too much to do. There is boredom, which we want to avoid at all costs. And there is our dislike of discomfort. If we start to look at where our attention goes and when, we find that much distraction happens as an unconscious response to these states. Because anxiety, stress and not doing anything at all are uncomfortable, we turn to our devices, where a 'like' on our latest social-media post will give us an endorphin rush, or we go shopping, or, more dangerously, we find comfort in drugs or alcohol. In short, those internal challenges make it difficult for us to focus and we have got too used to relying on easy ways to avoid experiencing emotional discomfort.

This is where mindfulness is so valuable. The clarity we discussed in the last chapter cannot be of any benefit if we don't learn to manage our monkey minds. Gaining clarity of purpose is useful only if we tie our actions to it. Mindfulness helps us develop our ability to focus, which means we can then engage properly with that purpose and act upon it.

The good news is that we all have the capacity to train our brains. Neuroplasticity is the name given to the brain's ability to adapt in response to learning and experience, building synaptic connections to create new patterns of attention and behaviour.

In the calendar and time audit in Chapter I, we started the process of recognizing the gaps between intention and action. Attention is the way we close that gap, enabling us to live out our priorities. In this chapter, we can build on that awareness of purpose by honing our attention through mindfulness and learning to focus on what is important to us.

MINDFULNESS THROUGH MEDITATION

The best way to train in mindfulness is through meditation. We increase the grey matter in the regions of our brain associated with focus when we meditate. We create new neural pathways and strengthen existing ones. The more we *train* our attention, the more easily we are able to *pay* attention.

We may not think of the mind as a muscle, but there are similarities between the way meditation practice can strengthen our attention and the way soccer drills can strengthen our ability to perform physically. Developing grey matter and rewiring neural networks is analogous to how athletes fine-tune their physiology and capacity to draw on strength and precision in movement with the training of muscle memory.

Plus, improving our attention actually improves our physical capacity as well, which is why elite athletes often use meditation and visualization to ramp up their performance on the field.

Phil Jackson, who coached eleven NBA championship teams, deployed visualization as a key tool in coaching the Chicago Bulls and LA Lakers. He writes about the technique and its power in his book *Sacred Hoops*. He taught some of the most talented players of all time how to become even more effective through meditation and visualization practices. He also taught players like Dennis Rodman how to use the breath to manage stress and emotions. Michael Jordan described the role of visualization as central in his success; he would visualize where he wanted to be, what kind of player he would become, and focus on achieving this.

Let's consider the rescue operation that enabled the Thai boys to leave the cave. As one of the Navy SEALs involved described, there have been cave rescues and there have been diving rescues, each dangerous and challenging; but putting a cave rescue and a diving rescue together makes the mission exponentially more complicated and perilous. This complication made the success of the enterprise appear unlikely at best. The Navy SEALs and engineers had to have extreme focus and the ability to maintain calm in the face of pressure for the rescue to have any chance of succeeding.

Giving in to extremes is a common habit when we experience stress. When we are in a situation that is threatening, there is the issue at hand, and then there is the fear of what that issue might develop into – a much bigger problem. In our panic, the fear takes over completely.

Being resilient in the face of extreme pressure requires the ability to handle unpleasant physical sensations and the internal dialogue that interferes with our common sense and prevents us from reaching for the best solutions. If we give in to this internal dialogue, we end up catastrophizing and obsessing about worst-case scenarios.

Having well-trained responders who could problem-solve, metabolize their stress effectively and persevere under pressure was a critical component of the rescue operation.

After all, they had plenty to be worried about: drastic cave currents, terrible visibility, narrow passages they would have to squeeze through, the threat of further monsoon rains and, of course, getting the boys out of the cave alive and safe.

The ability to keep cool in the face of danger doesn't happen magically. It gets to the very basis of mindfulness, which is that, if we can we learn to de-identify with the stories our imagination is creating, then they will seem much less real and burdensome. We can remind ourselves that the worst-case scenario belief is just our imagination in overdrive, so we don't have to dwell on it or pursue it. Instead, we can focus our mind on the difficult experience at hand, as well as our reaction to it. Then we are able to avoid responding in ways that could make our situation worse.

Some of the divers had to spend a lot of time waiting, either on their own or in pairs, in air chambers every couple of kilometres along the cave system. Ivan Karadzic, stationed at a halfway point in one of the chambers, had to replace air tanks and guide the rescue divers through to the next chamber. Imagine what it must have been like for him to sit there, waiting for a diver to arrive with one of the boys, not knowing whether the boy would be alive or not. Imagine keeping your cool when all around you is silence, darkness and water. What did Ivan do? He meditated.

Meditation provides us with the tools to calm our bodies as well as our minds. It is not surprising, then, that, for Buddhists, meditation is a go-to when they are distressed or in danger (not unlike how people from an Abrahamic tradition might default to prayer when they are in a life-threatening situation).

Many people don't realize that the basic principles of meditation are so easily accessible. Although it takes time to master, in order to gain enlightenment, it is not a complex skill to learn (as my Afterword shows). Coach Ekkapol could teach the boys quickly and efficiently, having meditated regularly for ten years. Breath-focused meditation – resting attention on the sensation of air entering and exiting the body – is a common method of meditation in Thai Buddhism and has calming effects on the body as well as the mind. It was exactly what they all needed, under the circumstances.

MEDITATION AND BUDDHISM

Meditation is at the very heart of Buddhism, and, with ninety-five per cent of Thais being Buddhist, it is an important aspect of the country's culture. Every year, for example, around one million children from five thousand schools convene at a Buddhist temple for a day of meditation for world peace.

Many believe meditation leads to happiness – indeed, Buddhist states of extreme concentration are described as blissful. In these states, the habitual recycling of concerns about the past, which is over and can't be changed, and fears about the future, which is yet to come and can't be controlled, becomes irrelevant. Much of traditional Buddhist practice is designed with these very human but ultimately unhelpful and unhealthy tendencies in mind.

Meditation is a form of mental training, a mechanism that forces meditators to focus, which leads to the rewiring of the neural networks. The more you do it, the better you get at it. In fact, the Tibetan word *gom*, which means 'meditation', can also be translated as 'familiarization'. The key is to do it regularly.

The right attitude is critical. We discussed the intention and attention earlier, but the mindset is also crucial. The attitude that best supports the development of mindfulness is curiosity. Can we be curious about our experience – even painful aspects of it – or, at a minimum, be non-judgemental? If the answer is yes, it allows us to experiment, to give it a try, to practise and persevere. It is when we are not self-critical or perfectionist that the growth happens.

The point of the meditation is to learn how to see, think and act in the world without being compelled by habits that may or may not be of service. Manage what you are thinking about, manage what you identify with – your thoughts don't have to be true. If you engage with your mind in this way, your behaviour necessarily follows, and your life is different. The trick is to change how you construct the world – to renovate your life.

PRACTICE TIP

In Buddhist practice, all of life is split into two categories: meditation and post-meditation. We meditate to learn how to deal with life, not just for the sake of meditation. We take what we have learned on the cushion, off the cushion. We must not get stuck or get too comfy on the cushion. Practice should make a difference in our lives, in our resilience. New meditators often trip up because they forget to hone their skill in everyday life. If you can remember to practise while you are busy, distracted and in the thick of things, you will be propelled forward on your path to transformation. The wisdom of the teachers states that we are well practised when we can take the mindset we have developed through meditation outside the meditative space, into the rest of our lives.

MINDSET HACK

Small actions matter. Keystone habits can change a pattern of behaviour and have a disproportionately positive impact. If we take up the habit of monotasking, we can hone our attention in new ways. Even monotonous work can become an opportunity for training in concentration. Try setting a timer for twenty-minute increments when you work. According to research, this is the length of time we can stay focused. Monotask well, take a break, and repeat. In this way, we can train ourselves to anchor our attention where it needs to be and to stop before it has wandered. This, in turn, engenders the capacity for meta-cognition, or being aware of what is preventing us from getting the best out of life.

LIGHT LIFT PRACTICE

Spend five minutes each day on this simple meditation, which you can find as a guided practice at www.leahweissphd.com/bhavana/.

Rest your attention on a physical object that you have placed eight to fourteen inches in front of you. Sit in the simplicity of observing this object. Each time you notice your mind wandering, guide it back gently, as you would guide a toddler back on to the path after they had run off in excitement. Do not try to suppress thoughts or chase them away. Trust the anchor to do the work for you. This basic exercise trains you to stay focused and to recognize when you are becoming sidetracked.

CHAPTER III

Kāya-Bhāvanā: Embodiment

'The mind is pure and luminous by nature. It is defiled only by adventitious thoughts and emotions'

The Buddha

Our well-being is fundamentally connected to our bodies. We often forget that this is the case, but that doesn't make it less true or less important. Even when we neglect our bodies altogether, they don't forget us. The moment we are sick, hurt ourselves, receive a diagnosis or narrowly avoid an accident, the truth of our embodied existence returns to us quickly. When the boys were found in the cave by the rescue divers, the first concern they communicated was the fact that they were hungry.

But what if we can harness the power of our minds to determine how we experience things physically? How can we use our minds to influence the wellness and healing of our bodies? Alia Crum, a researcher in the psychology department at Stanford University, conducted an interesting experiment in this area, dubbed 'the milkshake study' by the press. In it, she demonstrated that if we tell ourselves a 300-calorie vanilla milkshake is in fact a 160-calorie health shake, our hunger hormones react accordingly, and their levels will not drop as significantly as they would if we told ourselves we were drinking a full-fat 600-calorie indulgent treat.

What we think matters. When we learn to change our narrative, our bodies can change too. And this can be crucial in our quest for our health and resilience.

WHY EMBODIMENT MATTERS

In the cave, hunger and other physical realities, such as suffocating darkness and an invasive dampness that caused one of the boys to develop a lung infection, had to be managed. Ekkapol knew that he could not let the soccer team succumb to despair, and that, instead, he had to encourage them to cling to hope. He knew that meditation would help them cope with the harsh realities of their environment, and that, if he could just get them to concentrate on breathing in and breathing out, it would have a beneficial impact on their bodies. As we know from scientific research, when someone meditates successfully, their breathing slows, their heart rate goes down, their metabolism decelerates, cortisol levels decrease, oxygen utilization diminishes and carbon dioxide emission drops – all absolutely vital for the boys as they sat trapped in a cave where the air quality was gradually getting worse.

If the coach could get them to meditate, he'd be able to nurture their fighting spirit and keep their morale up. Ekkapol might not have read about the milkshake study, but he was experienced enough to realize that the body and emotions aren't separate, that thoughts influence physical wellness, and vice versa.

The most fundamental change we can make with respect to leveraging the connection between our body and mind is to reconnect them through the simple and powerful tool of attention.

For training in mindfulness or emotional intelligence, we start by pairing our body and mind to each other, as we would our phones to the cloud, and each time they become disconnected, we relink them, again and again. When we get better at this pairing, not only do we become more relaxed and productive, we also become more able to connect with others and with our priorities.

Mindfulness of physical sensations is the primary path of meditation articulated in early Buddhism. During meditation, a self-scan of the body is encouraged, to identify any tightness, pain or soreness, and therefore locate the areas where we carry our stress. Noticing where the tension lies, rather than suppressing it, can help us to release it.

When I was nineteen, I went on my first silent ten-day meditation retreat in Nepal. During the two-hour sits, we weren't allowed to move, and initially I found the physical discomfort of being completely still for so long almost intolerable. But I soon realized that the more I reacted with anger and frustration to my discomfort, the more my body ached. Conversely, when I focused fully on the pain and accepted it as part of the experience of meditating, the pain went away.

Physical pain is part of human experience – always has been and always will be. But it is worth remembering that chronic pain is on the rise, linked to the prevalence of our sedentary lifestyles. It's become more pertinent than ever to recognize mindfulness as one of the most effective ways to combat our suffering when it comes to pain.

Further evidence of the benefits of meditation can be seen when we consider biological markers, which help us understand its effect on diverse physiological signposts, such as inflammation, antiviral response, telomere length and cortisol levels. Telomeres are the protective caps on the ends of the strands of DNA called chromosomes, which house our genome, and shorter telomeres are associated with stress and indicate a higher risk of disease. In young humans, telomeres are between 8,000 and 10,000 nucleotides long. However, although telomeres naturally shorten as we age, research has shown that long-term meditators have higher levels of telomerase activity. Telomerase is an enzyme that repairs and rebuilds telomeres, meaning that meditation will help to maintain telomere length, providing greater protection against the onset of disease.

Meditation, when combined with mindfulness, can also alleviate depression, anxiety or distress. Behavioural changes that eliminate harmful bad habits and instead create new positive ones can become a reality. As we become more mindful, we see how our attention and beliefs influence our physicality and vice versa, and our emotional intelligence becomes more sophisticated.

The same is true outside of meditation, when we pay close attention to the information we and other people give out through non-verbal communication. Allowing ourselves to notice other people's physical behaviour when they are speaking to us enables us to pick up much more about what they are actually thinking. I learned, in my training as a therapist, to pay attention not only to what people were telling me, but also to their non-verbal communication. There is a lot to learn in this somatic dimension of our experience.

We receive many impressions in our day-to-day encounters with people that we can reflect back in potentially helpful ways. One way to work with this is to be aware of our own physical reactions to other people, such as an increase in respiration, pulse, or tension in the body. Noting how we physically respond in any social situation can provide a cue for how to behave, and it enables us to become more curious about the cause of these physical sensations. When we become more attuned to our patterns of response, we notice when our bodies are reacting to another person, so we can learn about ourselves as well as tune in to what the other person needs. Mindfulness helps us reclaim missing data in our experience, and in turn serves to improve all aspects of emotional intelligence, so we are able to relate skilfully to our own emotions as well as those of others.

Valuing the body's knowledge (including its needs and emotions) can offer up a first-class ticket to an understanding that comes with immense perks.

WALK WHILE YOU WALK, SIT WHILE YOU SIT

When the Buddha was asked by a student to summarize the essence of the Buddhist path to enlightenment, he answered that Buddhist monastics know when they are walking, eating and sleeping. The student was underwhelmed with the answer until the Buddha pointed out that, without a great deal of training, the default reality for most people is that they are not aware of what they are doing while they are doing it.

We live in a time of intense distraction, and there is little in the way of education that supports the value of an awareness of our bodies. Today, technology is designed to capture our attention, and many of us lack the basic skills that enable us to identify what we are feeling physically or emotionally at any moment, so the challenge of attention management has never been more urgent.

We are distracted and lose awareness of our purpose and attention much too easily. And when we don't know what we are thinking, our words can become harmful. When we don't know what we are feeling and why we are feeling it, our emotions can overwhelm us. This is why embodiment is one of the key principles of mindfulness. An ability to recognize subtle physical and emotional patterns is one of the essential signs of an accomplished practitioner.

We carry our physical and emotional history in our bodies. There are certain signs we can learn to recognize using mindfulness, such as the patterns surrounding a panic attack or a flare-up of sciatica. They are like triggers, or like a poker player's tells during a game. We can learn to harness these triggers to protect ourselves from trauma by leveraging self-knowledge and drawing upon the resources it gives us.

Being in the body is a key piece of training, and it takes practice. We know this from the world of sport. For example, we practise drills to identify our weak points (a slower backhand in tennis, or a left foot that's not as strong as a right foot in soccer) in order to make them stronger. Remember, the body and mind are not separate. Working on improving the self physically will resonate in the mind, and that which affects the mind has an impact on the body. As we saw in the previous chapter, elite athletes train in visualization, which influences their physical performance.

Another crucial aspect of mindfulness is developing body memory. Mental training can enhance the performance of hard-core physical tasks. In interviews, the divers who rescued the boys from the cave described not only mentally preparing for the operation, but also physically practising all the elements of the rescue ahead of time. They did not just think about it and write out the steps, but they rehearsed picking up and dropping off key pieces of equipment, such as the air tanks, on the way into the cave and then again on the way out, bearing in mind that, when the time came, they'd have the added challenge of a boy strapped to their body. They even created a miniature mock-up cave in a car park, so they could familiarize themselves with the various routes to where the boys were waiting.

Such rehearsal is common practice in training for military operations: layers of increasing complexity are added one step at a time, so that, when a person is caught up in the mayhem of a battle or a mission, they have cognitive as well as embodied recognition. This is consistent with the idea that people who are elite at anything need 10,000 hours of training to perfect it.

Training the mind helps develop intuition, too. Nobel-prize winner Daniel Kahneman describes this phenomenon in his book, *Thinking, Fast and Slow*, in which he demonstrates that, while we do have rationality and behave accordingly, we are also much more emotion led than we perhaps realize, often falsely claiming that our choices are the product of logical, careful thinking. Breaking this down further, he gets into subtle questions about how people who are elite performers, such as a fire chief, employ the non-rational information they have integrated from their experience. Again, we find they have learned to see patterns. As Kahneman puts it, 'intuition is recognition', which is especially true in physical circumstances, as for example in the case of the fire chief who knew to empty the burning building moments before it exploded because of the sensations he felt in his ears. He had intuitively recognized that something major was awry.

We too can learn to train ourselves to recognize patterns and signs of when things are aligned or askew.

CONNECT WITH YOUR BODY

Buddhism provides several perspectives on our relationship with the body.

One is renunciation, which includes overcoming attachment to our own body or to the bodies of others by understanding that the body is impermanent and, at some point, will die. Some practitioners might even sit with a decaying corpse during meditation to drive home the point that bodies are transitory and fleeting. An antidote to physical attraction or lust is to reflect on the innards of the body – the organs, or the contents of the stomach and bowels. The idea is that repulsion can help engender renunciation.

At the other end of the spectrum, some Buddhists feel that the body is a crucible for awakening. Buddhism encompasses the full range of human experience, and so the recognition of the nature of bliss – as in sensual experience, for example – can be seen as a direct path to awakening. In other words, paying attention to the details of physical pleasure can provide an analogue, or way in, to the direct experience of the blissful nature of our minds. Enlightenment, after all, is an experience that is profoundly joyful, and we need to learn to access that joy in sensation as part of our journey. From this point of view, we can train in practices like mindfulness of the body, or more advanced practices from Buddhist teachings, to learn the key lessons about the nature of mind and phenomena.

No matter which of these points of view we hold, we need to have a connection with our bodies. For many, this means moving away from a judgemental relationship of viewing the body as 'other' or as an object that is scrutinized and criticized. (Are my thighs too big? I wish I had thinner arms.) A neglectful relationship, paying attention to the body only when strictly necessary, is also unhealthy. Those who become disconnected from their bodies may not hear the messages it sends, leaving them vulnerable to being hijacked by whims such as overconsumption. This can lead to digestive issues, obesity, insomnia and chronic pain. Being disengaged in this way can result in fundamental disarray.

Learning to listen to what the body is telling us, and the ensuing knowledge that this offers, is the first step towards healing and wholeness. We can relearn what real hunger feels like; we can understand clothes from a functional point of view. Resisting the temptation to objectify the body and being grateful for its potential rather than being judgemental of it are the first steps towards enlightenment.

THE IMPORTANCE OF WORKING WITH EMOTIONS

Some may misconstrue mindfulness as dissociating from our bodies, arguing that thinking of our physicality stops us from being spiritual. But it is the opposite. Embodied mindfulness means having a profound intimacy with the experience of having a body. It means going beyond chasing pleasure all the time and avoiding anything we feel is difficult, uncomfortable or boring in our daily experience, and training ourselves to stay anchored in all of our sensations, thoughts and emotions, whether they be pleasant or unpleasant. This leads to acceptance-based equanimity with the body, with the mind and, therefore, with life.

For the boys in the cave, the ability to be aware of their fear and other strong emotions was critical. They had to accept their physical discomfort and acknowledge it while they were meditating, which allowed them to regulate their emotions and keep going. They were practising what is known as 'embodied mindfulness' in Buddhist psychology. Like these young boys, you too can learn emotion regulation as a skill. The best way to do this is to be mindful of your emotions rather than suppressing them.

MINDSET HACK

When feeling something uncomfortable emotionally or physically, do the opposite of what at first might seem logical. Lean in, get curious and pay attention. Don't be distracted or ignore feelings, and don't simply try to get rid of the pain. Remember that physical and emotional pain are part of life, and if you postpone engaging with the pain, you are putting yourself at higher risk of not being ready when the moment of dire need happens.

Follow Willy Wonka's advice to strike that and reverse it with your usual responses. Practise now. Don't wait till it is more convenient or you are in a better mental state. That day will likely never come. Practising now means getting better at it now, so that you are ready when you need these skills most. That's what Coach Ekkapol did for ten years in that temple.

LIGHT LIFT PRACTICE

Think of a current frustration in your life. Take a few moments to recollect the context. Try to get yourself into the experience of the frustration. How does it feel in your body? What kind of emotions are you experiencing? Start by resting your attention in your feet and slowly scan, with your attention, up to the top of your head. Notice the sensations you are experiencing as you move through the various parts of your body. Then scan back down to your feet again. Repeat this process for about five minutes.

This exercise will help you accept any unpleasantness you have been carrying with you in your heart and your mind.

CHAPTER IV

Mettā-Bhāvanā: Compassion

'May I be a protector for those who are without
protectors, a guide for travellers, and a boat, a
bridge and a ship for those who wish to cross over'

Shantideva, *A Guide to the*
Bodhisattva Way of Life

Devotion to the power of cultivating intentional mental states such as loving kindness would have been a crucial piece of Coach Ekkapol's training in the monastery. He would have spent thousands of hours studying the topic and practising.

Buddhists mean something specific by the term 'compassion'. In this chapter, we examine exactly what compassion is: caring when loved ones are struggling, and wanting to alleviate their suffering. *Metta*, which means 'loving-kindness', and compassion are taught together, and if you ask Buddhist teachers they make the point that despite the two words being distinct, they are synergistic in practical application. They both involve recognizing or being mindful of suffering and being willing to engage with that suffering when we see it. The point is, if we close our eyes to the suffering of others, or don't want to engage with suffering when we see it, or if we fear that we don't have the resources to be able to help, compassion becomes blocked.

Compassion is integrated within the practice of meditation – it is not purely conceptual. For those who expect meditation to be about sitting still and not thinking or feeling, this may come as a surprise. The meditations that train in the capacity for compassion are active. They include visualizing extending light from one's body to represent compassion, alongside mental recitations of phrases like, 'May you be happy,' or, 'May you be free of suffering.' Affirmations are traditionally used to support the practitioner in seeing other people as 'just like me' and building compassion. Other examples of common visualizations include the *tonglen* or 'giving and taking' meditation which draws suffering from others, visualized in the form of a dark fog or cloud that is transformed into compassion, healing and relief, and which is extended as a bright light directed towards the suffering party.

For Buddhists, love and compassion are core qualities that move them towards enlightenment. In Thailand, it is common to find diverse representations of the Buddha expressing various qualities of enlightenment, including compassion, and there are depictions of the prior lives of the Buddha (Jātakas) that exemplify this characteristic before he was reborn where he attained enlightenment.

In other Buddhist cultures, particularly Tibet, there is diverse iconography depicting archetypes associated with the qualities of enlightenment. Green Tara, for example, is a nurturing, protective, compassionate figure, and Chenrezig, of whom the Dalai Lama is understood to be an incarnation, is the Buddha of Compassion.

Practitioners pray to these images, use them as inspiration and employ them in visualizations as part of meditation practice. Experienced practitioners are capable of drawing on compassion at will and even in the most challenging circumstances. For example, the Dalai Lama often talks about Tibetan monastics who were captive in Chinese prison camps and used the opportunity to train themselves in compassion, even though they were experiencing torture and had minimal access to basic resources like food.

THE MUSTARD-SEED EFFECT

There was a woman in ancient India by the name of Kisāgotamī who suffered great tragedy. Her husband and children died, one by one, and when she lost her last child, she also lost her mind. A concerned neighbour took her to talk to the Buddha. Kisāgotamī hoped that, with his spiritual power, the Buddha could somehow rouse her dead baby, and so she carried it to him in her arms. The Buddha calmly listened to her story, then he told her to go back to the village and knock on each door until she could find a family that was not suffering from any kind of loss. When she found such a family, she was to ask them for mustard seeds, which she should collect and then return immediately to the Buddha.

Kisāgotamī went knocking from door to door, but at each stop the people who greeted her said they were unable to help. Each had lost a child, a parent or another family member. Eventually, after trying and trying, she returned to the Buddha having recognized that loss is a universal part of the human condition. This does not mean that the pain doesn't hurt, but the common experience of sorrow, loss and grief can open the door to an understanding of our shared pain and our shared need for resilience. On the heels of this realization, Kisāgotamī was ordained as one of the first Buddhist nuns to devote her life to meditation and awakening.

This mustard-seed effect – the recognition, through our suffering, of the universal reality of suffering – is the most potent foundation for expanding compassion within our immediate circle. It supports our willingness to extend compassion beyond that circle, to include people we don't know, enabling us to identify with them along the way. And eventually, we can expand our capacity to extend compassion to people we don't like, or even, like the example of the Tibetans extending compassion to the Chinese prison guards, to the people who harm us.

Don't get me wrong, this is a long process, and, having spent much of my own life working with trauma survivors and teaching compassion practice to them, I know how hard it is. I've worked with veterans with post-traumatic stress disorder (PTSD), including a man who was under supervised care because he had threatened his neighbour with extreme violence. After practising compassion meditation, he had a breakthrough in how he perceived the neighbour and was able to manage his own anger. When and if we are ready, techniques are available to help us develop the qualities of compassion in our daily lives, changing what we believe is possible in terms of our attitudes towards and thoughts about others.

A PATH TO HAPPINESS

One of the most interesting findings about the neuroscience of compassion comes from the study of the brains of meditation adepts. Brian Knutson, a neuroscientist and psychologist at Stanford University, put a group of Tibetan monastics into his imaging machine and asked them to do compassion meditation, as described in the visualization above. Compassion meditation is typically more active, using visualization and analytical thought as opposed to resting the mind on the simplicity of sensory perception. Knutson learned that this mental activity caused the reward regions of the brain to light up. This reaction is consistent with the experience compassion practitioners describe: compassion is a path to happiness. Engaging with suffering and connecting to a desire to support others engenders our own experience of well-being, which may seem counterintuitive. Surely, being immersed in suffering is depressing, so the natural instinct is to run away. But, instead of responding with distress, if we can learn to respond to suffering with compassion, then everyone benefits.

Compassion is often misunderstood. It does not mean throwing a pity party, opening our wallet to everyone who asks, or just nodding our heads in sympathy. Compassion means we uphold the potential in someone when their own stories or actions are causing them harm. Compassion helps us see beyond a person's behaviour to try to understand how their behaviour relates to their pain, goals and what's bothering them, and we are willing to speak difficult truths to help them realize their best selves. This approach allows us to speak our truth *and* to do so with love. It is a tremendous strength, and means we can relate to other people's anguish and points of view.

Compassion is a powerful force in generating and expressing wisdom, and cultivating it means developing your power as a person, leading to positive experiences and psychological states.

Buddhist psychology also notes the significance of the people around us in supporting our positive goals (like enlightenment). That's why community is one of the Three Jewels, alongside the Buddha and the teachings. Showing compassion to those around us strengthens the bonds of community, which is important because the tribe we choose or find ourselves in exerts such a strong influence.

ALTRUISM AND COMPASSION

Tellingly, compassion was evident at every turn during the Tham Luang rescue operation. For example, Ekkapol gave the few snacks he had with him to the boys. According to the divers, when they were discussing who was to be rescued first, the boys wanted those among them who lived furthest away to leave the cave first, so they could get home to their families at the same time as those who lived closest. There were Thai Navy SEALs who stayed with the boys, supporting and caring for them, and were the last out, further risking their lives the longer they stayed in that cave. This is the definition of altruism, or incurring self-sacrifice to support the well-being of another.

Evolutionary psychologists are pursuing this line of thinking more fully by examining compassionate characteristics developed across cultures and by exploring the physiological benefits of compassion for individual health. Organizational psychologists are decades into capturing how these processes of compassion play out in work situations; for example, they study compassion's effects on metrics such as a company's bottom line and performance, as well as its effects of employee engagement and retention. Across the board, compassion brings great results.

There are examples throughout history and around the world of people applying compassion as prisoners, even in the face of outright torture. And there were people in concentration camps and in other terrifying circumstances who, no matter how bad it got and when there was nothing in their surroundings to evoke it, retained their compassion.

Of course, we know that, from an evolutionary point of view, we have the capacity for altruism and the type of prosocial behaviour that helps others in our tribe. As Darwin said, 'Sympathy will have been increased through natural selection; for those communities which included the greatest number of the most sympathetic members would flourish best, and rear the greatest number of offspring.'

There is something reassuring and gratifying in knowing that it's in our DNA to feel empathy. But it is not a simple story, as a quick look at the news shows. It seems that we are willing to do a lot for our tribe or in-group, but we are much stingier when it comes to people we don't identify as being among our closest kin. Either of these impulses can become activated, and often we don't make this choice consciously. Our environment can nudge us in important ways, and it can be the deciding factor in our choice. Studies on oxytocin, the love hormone that is released in new mothers to help them cope with the sleeplessness involved in caring for helpless infants, show that, when we are given oxytocin around people we are close to, we experience feelings of love and connection. But when we receive it around people who are not in our in-group, we actually experience aggression.

Similarly, in the famed 1971 prison experiments at Stanford University, conducted by Phil Zimbardo, Stanford undergraduates were cast as prisoners and captors, with the whole exercise staged in the basement of the psychology department. The upshot was that, when put in these extreme conditions, within a matter of days, the undergraduates acting as captors were giving the 'prisoner' students shocks of electricity that, had they been real, would have been lethal.

We have the ability to transcend our environment if we choose, and training and determination can help us do this. These days, Zimbardo, now in his eighties, researches heroes and whistle-blowers to try to better understand what it takes to be a positive outlier who stands for truth, peace and compassion. One of his conclusions is that people who have trained and are mentally prepared ahead of time are more likely to behave with integrity. He studies former terrorists or gang members who become peace activists, and aims to understand the driving elements of their narrative and to identify themes across these exceptional people's stories.

PUTTING OTHERS FIRST

The boys' experience in the Tham Luang cave brought up evidence of compassion from several different angles. There was the compassion from the divers, who were prepared to risk their lives to help the coach and his team. Some have described it as a kind of wired-in condition – they couldn't *not* jump in when the need for their help was so crucial, when there were so many young lives at stake. Dr Richard Harris, the Australian anaesthetist who proved to be so instrumental in the rescue operation, cancelled his holiday immediately when he received the call about the boys trapped in the cave. Not only that, but he knew that his reputation and career were at stake if he didn't give the boys the right level of ketamine to keep them asleep while the divers swam with them to safety. One of the divers in the rescue operation, who carried numerous children on his back through the flooded passageways and tunnels, spoke about having intentionally hit his head a dozen times against the cave walls to protect the boys' skulls from cracking open on the ceiling. It is a tragedy that one person did die during the rescue effort, the retired Thai Navy SEAL, Saman Kunan. This level of selfless response corresponds to the positive-psychology research that the path to happiness is not to pursue our own pleasure, but actually to put others first.

In addition, there was compassion from observers around the world, as they stared at their computer and television screens with bated breath as the mission unfurled. What did this event mean to people so far away? With all sorts of other things to focus on, all the other tragedies in the world – such as starving people, violence, sex trafficking – why was this so mesmerizing and compelling?

It seems that we could all identify with the children, with the rescuers, with the families. An important topic in the study of compassion is compassion collapse. We know that people struggle to manifest compassion when the need is perceived to be more immense than our ability to respond to it. When we see one starving child on our television screens, we pull out our chequebooks, but when we see a thousand starving children, we shut down. Perhaps the fact that it was twelve boys made it possible for people to feel compassion in the way they did. Whatever it was, judging from the outpouring of comments on social media, everyone cared enormously about the boys' predicament.

And, after the rescue, the boys themselves showed how much they appreciated the compassion they'd received. In the *20/20* interview on the ABC network, the boys were overcome with tears of gratitude for the caregivers who had helped them. On Ellen DeGeneres' show, they spoke about their gratefulness for how much strangers from all around the world seemed to care for them while they were trapped.

The boys' parents were very supportive of Ekkapol. Instead of berating him for having taken their sons into the cave, they wrote letters, which were delivered by the divers, telling him that they were praying for him and thanking him for looking after the boys. They knew he was keeping them alive by getting them to meditate. Where other parents might have been struggling with conflicting emotions and finding it hard to forgive the coach, the Thai boys' parents were finding the compassion in their hearts to thank him and encourage him in his endeavours.

MINDSET HACK

When someone is bothering you, try to picture them as a person in their own right, with a whole life outside of the current situation. They are likely to have people who love and rely on them, who are invested in them financially, emotionally and physically. Also keep in mind that whatever they are doing that you don't like is perhaps a bid to meet some need that you may not understand, but that is significant to them. It is also helpful to tell yourself, 'This person is like me,' in that, like you, they make mistakes and are imperfect. We all have our weaknesses, after all. A dose of humility can go a long way to building bridges of understanding, and we can all benefit from remembering those times we acted like a jerk, not because we were bad people, but because we were under stress or had some other need or fear influencing us.

LIGHT LIFT PRACTICE

Ask a neighbour, friend or co-worker that you know is struggling how they are doing. Listen to their answer with your full attention. Nurture the relationship and build on it with two further gestures this week: ask them how they are doing again a few days later, and show that you were actually listening the first time by asking a follow-up question on a specific aspect of the situation they shared. Get them a coffee or tea when you get yours, and drop it off for them. It may not sound like much, but it is these small actions that can add up to a more compassionate attitude towards the self and others.

CHAPTER V

Paññā-Bhāvanā: Wisdom

'Meditation brings wisdom, lack of meditation leaves ignorance. Know well what leads you forward and what holds you back, and choose the path that leads to wisdom'

The Buddha

And now we get to the last and most important *bhāvanā*. It represents the culmination of all the other *bhāvanās*, all the trainings that we have been exploring so far. It is the *bhāvanā* of wisdom, or the realization of the ultimate non-dual state, which means you are embodying enlightenment.

The wisdom that emerges when you acknowledge the truth of mortality is the realization of the preciousness of life. In some sense, the choice the soccer team made, once they had left the hospital (where they stayed for a week, post-rescue, to avoid infection), to spend time at a Buddhist monastery as part of a novice-monk ordination process, was an acknowledgement of this wisdom. They stepped out of the media spotlight and spent nine days in the monastery. To go and practise there was a way to express gratitude by making the greatest possible use of the lives they were so lucky to have been spared. Or, as one of the rescuers put it, 'gratitude that they survived something they probably shouldn't have survived'.

To press pause, to take time away from the daily grind and to be open to having habitual perspectives challenged or questioned is crucial in the Buddhist tradition. Renouncing, for short periods of time, the focus on material fulfilment and on the comfort of routines, and to spend this time developing wisdom is the real entry to the Buddhist path of enlightenment.

RETREAT

Thai Buddhism has a long tradition of yogis retreating to the forest or a cave to practise, dating back to the time of the Buddha, 2,500 years ago. Retreat enabled them to work on deepening their wisdom, without any distraction. These forest monastics ate little – only two small meals between dawn and noon, which were offered by villagers as they wandered past when they left the forest – and they had few possessions. The monks were celibate and took vows not to handle money, which is why they relied on the generosity of their neighbours. They also had to develop strength of character, including the courage to cohabit with snakes and tigers and to endure the elements in the forest. The tradition is still alive today in north-eastern Thailand.

What do they do with their time in these natural surroundings? First and foremost, they take refuge by starting each day chanting: *Buddhaṃ saraṇaṃ gacchāmi, Dhammaṃ saraṇaṃ gacchāmi, Saṅghaṃ saraṇaṃ gacchāmi*. This translates from the ancient Pali language as, 'I go for refuge to the Buddha, to the truth of the way things are, and to the community.' They affirm this daily to avoid falling prey to the suffering of buying into meaningless obsessions in an overwhelming world. Then they spend their time working on the very practices that we have discussed in this book, the *bhāvanās*.

One of Tibetan Buddhism's most famous cave yogis, Milarepa, who was born in the eleventh century and who is often depicted in Tibetan art as slightly green because of living in caves and subsisting on a diet predominantly featuring nettles, summed it up neatly: 'When you realize your mind, you become a Buddha. It is unnecessary to talk and do a lot! There is no other teaching more profound than this. Follow and practise, then, all these instructions.'

Of course, it's not realistic for most people to think of taking time out in a cave or a forest. That would be a bit of an ask. Nor is it always easy to take a week in a Buddhist monastery in Thailand, although that could, of course, be beneficial. Instead, consider spending a weekend in a nearby silent retreat, or if that is too impractical, just focus on building one meditation session into each day.

WHAT WILL WISDOM BRING?

Wisdom allows us to recognize what Buddhists call the Eight Worldly Winds, which are Pleasure and Pain, Gain and Loss, Praise and Blame, and Fame and Disrepute. These hopes and fears hijack a large percentage of our available mental bandwidth: hope for happiness and the fear of losing it; worrying whether we'll be rewarded or shunned; whether we'll be famous or irrelevant; and whether we'll gain or lose material wealth. It isn't to say that we don't need some of these concerns in our life, but they can preoccupy us to such an extent that they take over completely. For many of us, there will never be enough pleasure, wealth, recognition, adulation, and the problem is that we risk becoming crippled by the lack of contentment.

The point of the *bhāvanās* is to gain wisdom that will allow us to understand our habits and the way we rely on patterns of constructing reality in unproductive ways. We relearn how to see, how to stay connected with the crucial purpose of our lives, how to be in our bodies rather than lost in our minds, and how to connect to the elixir of compassion. These practices help us understand that all things are interdependent, and that our ideas, the events we experience and the people around us are not always as they appear to be.

The good news is that wisdom is in each and every one of us. It is innate, but we can't access it when we are distracted and confused. The *bhāvanās* help us cut through our mental clutter. Common traditional metaphors used to depict enlightenment include a buddha covered with mud and a diamond buried beneath the hovel of a destitute person.

This idea of hidden layers and veils being parted is present in other traditions. It is found in the use of sacramental substances in the Christian tradition, for example, as a means to connect with 'the really real', as my former professor, Father Michael Himes, put it. The metaphor of illumination, or the ability to see (as opposed to being entangled in the darkness of ignorance), is another common framing, used across religious traditions.

The power of visualization – deconstructing and reconstructing reality – dovetails with research being done on the power of the mind and how our beliefs about the foods we eat, the medicines we take and even the stress we experience influence how healthy or sick we become. This understanding can lead to a new level of self-efficacy where we can take responsibility for our actions and flex the beliefs we hold.

KARMA

Recognition is an interesting concept in the context of the Thai cave rescue. It was evident from the interviews with the rescue divers that they weren't risking their lives to achieve fame. A lot was at stake; after all, the odds didn't look good, with those in charge of the operation saying that they anticipated at least some of the boys would die during the rescue mission. How can you be thinking of the prospect of fame when you might be the one carrying out a child that dies, and you have to live with that?

Buddhists don't believe in fame, but they do believe in merit or positive karma, which is one of the reasons they take giving and receiving offerings so seriously. They feed the wandering forest monastics or place fruit and cookies in front of a statue of Buddha because they believe it will bring them positive karma. In Chiang Rai province, while Ekkapol and the boys waited in the cave, their families made offerings of flaming candles to the Buddha in nearby temples. Among them was Tum Kantawong, Ekkapol's godmother, who regularly appealed with fruits, incense and candles to Jao Mae Nang Non, the princess whose guardian spirit is said to protect Tham Luang cave and the surrounding mountain. Another offering came from a Thai monk, who made bracelets and blessed them before giving them to the Navy SEALs. Countless Thais prayed for the boys' rescue, and, in many ways, while prayer is reassuring to the self, it is also a form of offering to others.

But, in another situation, would the fact of wanting

recognition devalue the altruistic act? Are the ideals that we need to uphold so pure and so good that, as soon as mixed motives enter the picture, the good deeds are invalidated? How untainted *do* our motives need to be? We must use discernment to determine what is true and false, what will lead us in the direction we want to go and how to navigate complexity. Often, in life, there are no clear or easy answers, and drawing on meditation and the knowledge it yields can help us to become wiser and live a happier life.

OPEN-FOCUS

In open meditation, we don't focus on an object or the breath so much. Instead, we let the mind take us where it wants to, and we allow any emotion or thought or feeling to bubble up to the surface. In this state, we can ask ourselves the big questions: Who am I? Where is my volition? Where does my identity come from?

The ability to recognize and rest in this awareness is the cornerstone of wisdom. Researchers such as Lorenza Colzato have investigated open-focus meditation and observed how it allows us to connect ideas. Essentially, she has found that this open monitoring practice supports what cognitive psychologists call 'divergent thinking', or the connecting of ideas, which is a key ingredient of creativity. This type of meditation in a sense replicates what happens when someone has been working on a problem, perhaps for months or years, and the solution clicks into place when they are doing something else. Open-focus meditation allows 'aha' moments to emerge, enabling us to become more creative and better at problem solving when we learn this technique.

There is a schema that helps us take the new head-knowledge we have, integrate it into our meditation, and from there apply it to all that we do. The schema is view, meditation and action. First, we need to align our thinking and decide what to take up and what to reject, understanding what wisdom looks like, so we know it when we experience it.

And we need to do a lot of practice, familiarizing of ourselves with the perspective through meditation. Then, we need to bring it forth to the rest of our lives through our actions.

MINDSET HACK

What could you do less of right now to free up greater spaciousness in your perspective? You might want to be silent more often, not insisting or advocating so much, or you might want to schedule less in your calendar. Even thinking about releasing the grip in the jaw or shoulders can work.

Can you find and carry the thread of awareness throughout your activities in your day?

Find one realistic in-between or interstitial spot in your life – after a workout, when you wake early to sip tea and look out the window at the sunrise – and savour this time. Notice your perspective and how it is different from how it is in other parts of your day. How can you create more of these micro-moments in your busy day to punctuate your life with space, with wisdom?

LIGHT LIFT PRACTICE

After you have taken a few deep breaths and done a focusing meditation, turn the mind towards itself. See if you can witness the process of the mind constructing reality – the chains of thoughts linking together – and, when you notice it, just stop chasing. De-identifying with a fixed sense of self and with our thoughts is the basis for the embodiment of wisdom. You can practise this in your daily life. Ask yourself, Who is there to chase? Who is the one witnessing? Who is wondering about the witness? Who wants the peaceful mind? Who wants to improve themselves? Who is afraid they can't or won't? Who is judging the meditation or experiencing the calm and peace. Who or what is doing all of this work? Who is exhausted? What is there beneath all of this? Who is the one seeing and hearing? What is the continuous aspect of all of this experience that unifies it?

Notice your response, and notice that your sense of identity may loosen up a bit, which gives you more of a sense of freedom in perspective. It helps make you less attached to your opinions about who you are, and your habitual thoughts. You may find that you are able to be more at ease.

AFTERWORD

My Meditation Guide

When I was nineteen, I went for the first time to Bodh Gaya, India, where the Buddha is said to have attained enlightenment under the bodhi tree. There were Buddhists from all over the world gathered at the main temple, wearing coloured robes of many styles and bowing in various poses. Some were full-body prone, throwing themselves down, then standing up and repeating this action, over and over. Others placed their knees, hands and the top of the head gently on the ground.

This was a key lesson to me. The fundamentals of a Buddhist practice remain consistent, but the way you create your own practice must suit you and fit in with the needs and patterns of your life.

This meditation guide contains tips, advice and ideas you can take with you as you set up your own personal practice. You will soon find out that the basic principles of meditation can be learned quickly – it is not a complex skill to learn, but it does take time to master.

A FEW FUNDAMENTALS

Many people have the idea that meditation will miraculously and instantly still the mind and get rid of all thoughts and feelings. They may begin to feel they are failing if they can't stop the activity in their brains, that they must be doing it wrong, that it's not for them. Then they might give up. But that is a mistake. As one of my meditation teachers,

Charles Genoud, would say, 'It is good if your mind wanders. It means you are not dead.'

Experiment with a few methods. Some people really resonate with a simple breath practice, but others do better with visualization or something more physically oriented. You can give yourself a grace period to try a number of methods a number of times and see what works best for you.

Apply the same principles to meditation as you would to starting any new habit or activity. Create a specific time and place for a regular practice. Set a realistic initial goal that you can succeed at and build from. Recognize that resistance to the habit and to the meditation itself is part of the process. So, having an accountability buddy, a system, or joining a class is helpful for many people. Some people like meditation apps, although classes are more effective, as research indicates.

As is emphasized throughout the book, you need to practise again and again. You will need to try it a number of times before it feels comfortable. This is normal. Don't feel like you can't meditate if you don't have a life-changing epiphany the first time you sit and try a practice. Traditionally, you would be sent off by your teacher to try an instruction a thousand times before you came back to debrief on what you'd learned.

The Buddha instructed that there are three ways to meditate: walking, lying and sitting down. Any of the practices in this guide can be done in any of these positions. Let's look for a moment at how to bring meditation and movement together.

Walking

The most straightforward version of a walking meditation is to rest your attention in your body while you walk. Feel each step as you pick one foot up, move it forward, plant it on the ground, and then repeat with the next one. You should feel your weight shift. You can slow down or walk at a regular pace, but the key thing is to keep your attention on your body's movement all the time. Be the walking, rather than the person who is walking and lost in their thoughts.

Of course, if you are walking down a busy street, it will be hard to block out the sights, sounds and smells around you. Notice what comes through, and where your attention gravitates towards, but always try to bring it back to what your feet are doing.

Lying Down

Meditation while lying down can be an extremely grounding practice (pun intended). Allow the surface you are lying on to hold you. Give over your weight to the ground and let it support you. If you are familiar with yoga, adopt the position of 'corpse pose' or *shavāsana*, which usually comes at the end of a yoga session – non-doing after doing.

This type of meditation is particularly effective when you get home from a long and stressful day at work. Let the tension of the day leave your body. Notice any places you feel tightness, but watch out for snoring meditation.

Sitting Down

Find yourself a seat that makes sense for you. The key to a practice is that you need to do it, so you don't want to set yourself up for physical pain that will stand in the way of doing your meditation session. Whether you sit on a chair, a cushion or a bench, the main point is to have somewhere you can be relaxed and upright. It can also be helpful to have a meditation shawl to wrap yourself in if you get cold or just want the comfort.

You can sit in a chair with your feet on the floor, or cross-legged on a cushion on the floor, keeping your back straight but not rigid.

MEDITATION RITUALS

We all need transition time. It is difficult to come in from a long, stressful day and just leap on to the meditation cushion. Rituals help us prepare ourselves; even if they might feel awkward initially, in time they can become an important means of expression. Below are descriptions of some of the traditional rituals that accompany meditation practice. There is no pressure to start any of them, or to try them in any particular order. But you can explore them in your own time and the information below will give you enough understanding of the underlying hows and whys to guide you.

Create an Altar

In its most essential form, creating an altar means creating a space for your practice. You certainly can meditate anywhere, but some people find it profoundly nurturing to create a specific zone for their meditation practice at home. It will become imbued with the inner feelings you generate in your practice and with the wisdom you access along the way.

Offering

Making an offering to the altar can take different forms. It could be that you light a candle, fill offering bowls with water or traditional substances that represent the senses, or you could put out fresh fruit or sweets. You could also light a stick of incense (representing smell), use musical instruments (representing sound) or put money on your altar, giving it away later to a charity or a homeless person you meet on the street. Creating beauty and delighting the senses, as an act of gratitude to the lineage of practitioners, to the weight of wisdom and to the many others who have walked the path before us, can be a source of connection and strength.

Bowing

A bow is a way to kick-start the process and acts as a sort of signal that you welcome the idea that whatever you encounter is significant, the experience you meet is your teacher. You can bow to honour the lineage of wisdom-holders, people who over time have committed to growing in truth, have learned to embody it and whose company you are joining. You can also bow to the other practitioners who are walking the path with you, if you are part of a class.

Buddhist Prayer

Devotion to the path and process of awakening, to the teachings and to the practice itself can take expression in the form of prayer. We can pray to uncover our inner wisdom or teacher, in the hope that it may elucidate our practice and lives. There are many beautiful prayers in the Buddhist tradition, but you can also bring in those from your own religion, or employ poetry that evokes for you the qualities of the *bhāvanās* you are developing.

Here is a traditional favourite that has been chanted by millions for over a thousand years:

May the brilliant sun of awakening
Dawn in every single heart–mind
Cutting through the darkness of anguish and
    confusion
Unstoppably until every being is awake and
    enlightened.

May all beings have happiness and the causes of happiness.
May all beings be free of suffering and the causes of
    suffering.

May all beings remain inseparable from the ultimate
happiness, which is devoid of suffering.
May all beings remain connected with boundless
equanimity, free from both excessive attachment to
loved ones and rejection of those they dislike or hate.

A SUMMARIZED GUIDED MEDITATION FOR THE FIVE BHĀVANĀS

In this section, we will combine the practices we've encountered so far and bring them together in one place. You will be reminded of the necessary methods to bring each of the five bhāvanās into your daily life through mindset, reflection and meditation. With practice, over time, you can develop each of these skills and increase your overall well-being as well as your resilience.

The **Light Lift** practices are what Buddhists refer to as 'off-cushion' tools. They are methods you can use in your daily life, so that you learn to integrate these principles into the way you approach your daily activities.

The **Mindset Hack** exercises are quiet meditations you can do that complement the integrated exercises.

You can customize your journey with these tools. You could take it from the top and work through each *bhāvanā* sequentially. For example, you might spend a week or a month focusing on the first *bhāvanā*, then move on to the next, and so on. Or, you might feel drawn to one particular concept to start with and begin with the *bhāvanā* that resonates the most with you.

Whichever method you choose, remember, these practices take practice. The more you do them, the more comfortable and skilled you'll become, and they'll be in your toolkit for evermore.

Bhāvanā One – Clarity/Purpose

Light Lift

With each new undertaking, clarify your intentions. In the midst of your activity, when you find your attention straying, remind yourself what you are doing.

Mindset Hack

In your meditation, consider that life is short and you don't know when it will end. One day, you might find yourself abruptly interrupted, and it is up to you to be ready. The best way to do that is to take each day seriously. If tomorrow is your last day, how would you want to spend it? If today is your last day, do you think it has been well used? Consider what you most want to contribute to the world, what you want to be remembered for at the end of your life. You have a precious opportunity to learn and contribute to the world. Reflect on what it would mean to you to use it well.

Bhāvanā Two – Focus/Attention

Light Lift

Take note of your breath. Pay attention to how it and your mind interact. When you feel stress or anxiety, how does this influence your breath? Take a few deeper breaths to help your body relax and your mind stop spinning.

Mindset Hack

Rest your attention on the object you are choosing for your practice. If you have chosen to focus on the sensations of the inhalation and exhalation of the breath, then place your attention on these sensations. Each time you notice the mind straying, gently return it to the anchor or to the breath.

Bhāvanā Three – Embodiment

Light Lift

When feeling something uncomfortable emotionally or physically, do the opposite of what at first might seem logical. Lean in, get curious, pay attention. Don't be distracted or suppress feelings or try to get rid of the pain. Remind yourself, this is what it means to feel this or that emotion, and this is part of what it means to be human. Follow Willy Wonka's advice to strike that and reverse it when it comes to your usual responses.

Mindset Hack

Think of a current frustration in your life. Take a few moments to recollect the context. Try to get yourself into the experience of the frustration. How does it feel in your body? What kind of emotions are you experiencing? Start by resting your attention on your feet and slowly scan your body, up to the top of your head. Notice the sensations you are experiencing as you move through the various parts of your body. When your attention reaches the top of your head, scan slowly down to your toes. Repeat this process slowly and deliberately for about five minutes. Set a gentle timer, if you like, to help you keep track.

Practise now. Don't wait till it is more convenient or you are in a better mental state. That day will likely never come. Practising now means you will be better at it later, so you will be ready when you need these skills most. That's what Coach Ekkapol did for ten years in that temple.

Practise now. Remember that physical and emotional pain are part of life, and postponing your practice of engaging with something that hurts you puts you at greater risk of not being ready when the moment of dire need arrives. Don't wait until it is more convenient or you are in a better mental state.

Bhāvanā Four – Compassion

Light Lift

Take the time to ask someone you know is struggling how they are doing. When they answer, slow down and really listen to them. Support this connection with two further gestures this week: follow up and check in a few days later, asking about some aspect of what they shared to show that you were actually listening and care, and grab them a cup of coffee when you pick one up for yourself. Small actions like this demonstrate our concern and build strong relationships.

Mindset Hack

Use daily annoyances as an opportunity to develop your compassion. When you are interacting with someone you dislike or who is annoying, intentionally recall texture to this person's life. Consider that there might be stressors – a loved one who is ill, or trauma from their past that is informing their behaviour. Also, it can be helpful to consider the person in the context of other relationships – picture them as a child, partner, parent – and consider that there are people in their life who rely on them. If they lack these relationships, this in itself may well engender compassion. Last, but not least, consider ways in which you yourself have demonstrated the kind of behaviours you are triggered by in this other person. All of these reflections will help reveal the perspective that this person is, in fundamental ways, 'like you' – we all make mistakes and are imperfect.

Bhāvanā Five – Wisdom

Light Lift

Wisdom is innate, not something that has to be created from scratch. This means that the most direct strategy to increase your wisdom is to strip away any obstructions preventing you from accessing it. Tactically speaking, look for places in your day where you can take a broader perspective. This can come in the form of creating interludes of silence, a willingness to question your own interpretation, or even clearing space in your calendar.

Mindset Hack

Wisdom meditation is the process by which we can experientially clarify how our minds and perception function. This is the path to catalyze glimpses of your innate wisdom.

Instead of focusing on chains of thoughts or external experience, turn the mind inward, towards itself. Investigate how thinking actually occurs. How do thoughts emerge? Where do they come from? How do you construct reality by creating and believing chains of thought? What happens when you stop chasing thoughts and allow them to arise and then dissolve, as a snowflake melts on a sun-warmed rock?

Don't try to change your experience – rest in the uncontrived awareness of your experience, without trying to become anyone or accomplish anything – simply be with whatever you are experiencing, with simplicity.

Without chains of thought and a strongly reified thinker, who is the person left? Who is aware of an active or clear mind? Who is wondering if they are meditating correctly? Who is the meditator? These are not philosophical questions to think about; they are instructions that are intended to guide your investigation.

SIGNS OF A MATURING MEDITATION PRACTICE

(based on a thousand-year-old mind–heart training text, *The Seven Points of Mind Training* by Chekawa Yeshe Dorje)

- You don't take yourself so seriously. Life overall becomes less of a rollercoaster. You are less in the grip of worry, anxiety and fear. You may well have thoughts that are anxious and fearful, but you don't feel compelled to believe them and enact the same stress-induced behaviours they motivate. As a result, you are finding more joy in your life.
- Your relationships are improving. You are more able to see other points of view. Even if you don't agree with them, you can recognize that another person has a history and their own rationale (or unmet needs) which will drive their ideas and behaviour.
- You are more able to deal with challenges by drawing on your practice. You might not be able to do so immediately, but you will get better at this as you train.

- You are accessing your own discernment in the decisions you are making in your life. You are drawing on your inner teacher and inner clarity.
- You are less judgemental of yourself and other people, or, at the very least, you recognize when you are being so.
- You aren't stuck in the same predictable habits. You are able to try something different in response to a stressful situation.
- You are changing your attitude, but are not acting like your spiritual awakening is a Very Big Deal.
- People are noticing something is different about you, but not because you are a zealot. You don't proselytize. You show them; you don't tell them.

Acknowledgements

Writing a book is a lot like having a baby. Inception can't happen alone, gestation tests patience, and labor is intense (to say the least). I'd like to thank my midwives in this project – Katy Follain at Quercus, my wonderful literary agent Stephanie Tade – and express immense gratitude to my dear friend, Jill Stockwell, who has accompanied me throughout this entire process with humor, wisdom, and incredible skill.

I would also like to thank my loving husband, David Ekstrom, for believing in me and making it possible for me to truly lean in to what I'm here to do in this world. To my children who inspire me every day in so many ways – you are everything to me. Beatrice Rose, our leader, you amaze me with your insistence on justice, your voracious appetite for knowledge, and your boundless joy. Caleb, my middle child, I'm immensely grateful for your huge, loving heart, your goofy sense of humor, and your astounding earnestness. To Isaac, the baby of the family, you are a fellow theologian and our conversations about the nature of life, death, and beyond mean the world to me.

I'd like to thank my mother, Madge Weiss, for always supporting me and for encouraging me to write, speak my mind, and dream big in terms of impact on the world. My siblings Jennifer and Adam Weiss, you are my best friends and I love and admire you both so much. Madeleine, Faye, Lila, Colette, and Ryan – I adore all of you and it is such a joy to be your aunt.

I want to thank you with my whole heart for your friendship, insight, and support: Pat Christen, Thupten Jinpa, Mary Oleksy, Amanda Mahoney Kuhn, Jennifer DeWitt, Monica Hanson, Margaret Cullen, Erika Rosenberg, Alena Skrbkova, Andrea Hermosura, Sarah Rushford, Dina Venezky, and all of my students at Stanford Graduate School of Business who have taught me so much.

I truly hope that this book provides benefit to all who read it.